JEREMY AND Mom

Also by Jerry Scott and Jim Borgman

Zits: Sketchbook 1
Growth Spurt: Zits Sketchbook 2
Don't Roll Your Eyes at Me, Young Man!: Zits Sketchbook 3
Are We an "Us"?: Zits Sketchbook 4
Zits Unzipped: Zits Sketchbook 5
Busted!: Zits Sketchbook 6
Road Trip: Zits Sketchbook 7
Teenage Tales: Zits Sketchbook 8
Thrashed: Zits Sketchbook No. 9
Pimp My Lunch: Zits Sketchbook No. 10
Are We Out of the Driveway Yet? Zits Sketchbook No. 11
Rude, Crude, and Tattooed: Zits Sketchbook No. 12

Treasuries

Humongous Zits
Big Honkin' Zits
Zits: Supersized
Random Zits
Crack of Noon
Alternative Zits

A ZITS® Retrospective You Should Definitely Buy for Your Mom

by Jerry Scott
& Jim Borgman

**Andrews McMeel
Publishing, LLC**

Kansas City

Zits® is syndicated internationally by King Features Syndicate, Inc. For information, write King Features Syndicate, Inc., 300 West Fifty-Seventh Street, New York, NY 10019.

08 09 10 11 12 BAM 10 9 8 7 6 5 4 3 2 1

ISBN-13: 978-0-7407-7101-9
ISBN-10: 0-7407-7101-9

Library of Congress Control Number: 2007937789

Zits® may be viewed online at
www.kingfeatures.com.

www.andrewsmcmeel.com

Our special thanks to Molly Choma for her help on the book design and
for her amazing patience with the !@*%# copy machine.

ATTENTION: SCHOOLS AND BUSINESSES

Andrews McMeel books are available at quantity discounts with bulk purchase for educational, business, or sales promotional use. For information, please write to: Special Sales Department, Andrews McMeel Publishing, LLC, 4520 Main Street, Kansas City, Missouri 64111.

For Peggy and Marian, who loved us anyway.
Your boys,
Jerry and Jim

Introduction

From Sophocles to Sigmund Freud, writers, philosophers, and psychoanalysts have attempted to unlock the code to the mysteries of the mother-son relationship. Nice try, boys. Popular culture, too, has taken its shot at this dyad in novels, film, and TV sitcoms. Off the mark. And then come Jerry Scott and Jim Borgman, preeminent lords of comic strip comedy, enlightening the world by bringing you the best of Jeremy and his mom in *Zits*. In just four boxes and minimal dialogue, under the guise of humor and sarcasm, these two savvy writers reveal the thoughts and feelings universal to teenage boys and their mothers.

For the past thirty years, I have been a family therapist guiding Los Angeles–area clients through the hilly terrain of family life. What I've heard over these past thirty years would blow your mind: parents doing drugs with their children, children deciding if and when they go to school, teenagers expecting to have their girlfriends sleep over after the keg party they had for their friends, and the list goes on. How do we deal with these inevitable messes? Sure, patience, understanding, and the occasional limit-setting tirade are all essential tools for dealing with the ups and downs we all encounter. But for my money, humor remains one of the most invaluable tools for a family to get through the day unscathed. Humor helps to diffuse tension and even allows us to lightheartedly respond to outlandish, adolescent requests: "Of course we'll leave the house for the weekend, honey, so you and your animal-like friends can trash the place . . . NOT!"

Humor is the vantage point from which the authors take aim at Jeremy awkwardly attempting to assert his independence, while his mother lovingly fumbles with her new role. We laugh at the interactions between Jeremy and his mom because we recognize ourselves, either as the self-involved adolescent living in the world of "now, now, now," or as the mother constantly trying to ride out the less-than-perfect storm. When I was a teenager back in Philadelphia, my whole family kept their distance from my dad and his nasty temper. The only place my mom was able to smoke a cigarette without my dad finding out about it was in the kid's bathroom. Every time she finished a cigarette, I slipped in behind her and had one myself. What a great cover! Scene after scene in *Zits*, we watch as Jeremy's need for independence runs smack into his need for his mother. Jeremy says it best when he thinks to himself that he wants to be "left alone, not ignored." Yet despite the bumpy road, Jeremy and his mom manage to hang on to each other, and we get to go along for the hilarious ride.

—Dr. Roy Ettenger, Ed.D., M.F.T.

Jim: *Zits* came to life on the porch of a cabin in Sedona, Arizona, in April 1996. From that first night when Jerry and I sat up talking about and sketching the characters, it was always clear that Jeremy and his mom would be at the heart of things.

Jerry: As characters were created, discarded, reshaped, or reborn, the central theme of this comic strip has remained unchanged; teenagers will drive you crazy.

Jim: I've raised two kids of my own, and then five years ago found myself in a new blended family with three more stepchildren—all five of them teenagers at once! I parked my drawing board in the middle of our family room, an embedded cartoonist, and just started writing down what I saw and heard. Jerry and I live in different parts of the country but we talk every day. I don't know how he does it, but he listens to my notes from the field, mixes them with heaping bucketfuls of his own magic, and spins gold.

Jerry: Of all the themes we explore in *Zits*, the relationship between Jeremy and Mom is the one I enjoy writing about most. I hear their voices more clearly than any of the other characters. The complicated mental and emotional push-pull between a mother and her son is (so far at least) an endless source of humor. From cellular mitosis through tripping over size 16 shoes strewn around the living room, it's a complicated, loving, tense, explosive, and undeniable bond that's best experienced with a healthy dose of perspective and humor. In a sense, what we do is just reassure readers that they're not alone. If it helps, you're welcome. Enjoy the book.

13

Jerry: I think some of the most successful ideas we've done contain visual gymnastics that no other art form does better than a comic strip. A drawing like the one on the left side of page 15 gets you inside Jeremy's head (and Mom's, too, I guess) quicker and better than ten pages of dialogue.

Jim: When I draw the Duncan family, I try to make Jeremy almost the same height as his parents to suggest a figurative competition for dominance. Walt generally wins by a hair, literally.

Jerry: I remember taking my mom and my mother-in-law to Mother's Day brunches like the one depicted in this strip. There's nothing we guys think a woman loves more than standing in line for an hour for the opportunity to consume huge amounts of institutional breakfast fare (scrambled eggs always taste best fresh from the vat). The reason men equate all-you-can-eat brunches with honoring one's mom is a subtle nuance of masculinity: you nourished us, now we nourish you . . . nearly to death. Women seem to have trouble understanding this.

Jim: We've settled on Mother's Day picnics in our family after one too many chocolate fountains.

Jim: In a couple of our early strips, we showed Mom as a child psychologist, but soon she settled into her role as a stay-at-home mom who is working on, and constantly interrupted from, writing a book. She'd be the proofreader in the family.

Jim: It's easy to do the sarcastic stuff. Capturing the warmer, playful moments is tougher.

Jerry: I love this strip. It's not the funniest one I've ever written, but I think it's the first time that we showed Jeremy and Mom being playful. In the midst of the daily grind, teenagers are often not credited for the sense of pure silliness they possess.

Jerry: For a long time this was my favorite *Zits* strip. You can almost hear the slam of the door in the split-second sitcom timing of the last panel. Well, at least I can.

Jim: Jeremy in a sweater vest. Yeah, that'll happen.

Jim: Besides doing *Zits*, I've been drawing editorial cartoons for the *Cincinnati Enquirer* for thirty years. Caricaturing people in the news is one of my great pleasures, so I love it when the rare opportunity pops up in *Zits*.

36

Jim: Uh-oh, suddenly the kid has a middle name. Hope we can remember it the next time the situation comes up.

Jerry: This, of course, is based on the famous Serenity Prayer used in many twelve-step programs. The idea came out of one of the thousands of non-cartoon-related conversations Jim and I have had that have been the richest source of material for the strip. Ever notice the disturbing similarities between parenting and recovery?

Jim: My son teases me about having once dusted the top of the basement refrigerator when he had his girlfriend over.

39

Jerry: I write comics with sort of a cinematic approach. I imagine a setting and characters for a scene, then start mentally pruning unnecessary detail and compressing or stretching time until the story can be told with the right pace. This one had to be stretched to depict all of the awkward silence of one of those one-way conversations every mom has had with a teenager.

Jim: As a grizzled cartoonist, only a few of your own strips make you laugh each time you see them. This is one of my all-time favorites.

41

Jerry: There was a lot of positive feedback on this strip. Something tells me that there must be other procrastination-prone teenagers out there.

Jim: We've tried to hold the line in our household, but the entertainment industry is not our ally in the battle.

Jim: Give the kid a couple more months and his legs will reach all the way over into *Garfield*.

Jerry: Stretching reality to illustrate a point about Jeremy's growth is a theme we revisit fairly often. The speed at which kids grow is hard to believe unless you keep a record of it. We started marking our kids' growth progress on one side of the casement around my studio door. When we moved last year, we took it with us.

50

Jim: We've talked about starting a comic strip about teenage girls because Jerry and I have four between us and it's a whole different universe. I didn't have to go far for reference material for this shower scene—just down the hallway to the bathroom my two daughters share.

54

Jerry: This is shamefully familiar to me. I'd hate to admit the percentage of the things my mom said to me that actually made contact with my brain cells.

Jim: OK, I don't know what I was thinking with Mom's sleeveless turtleneck. My daughters have demoted me to Remedial Fashion 101.

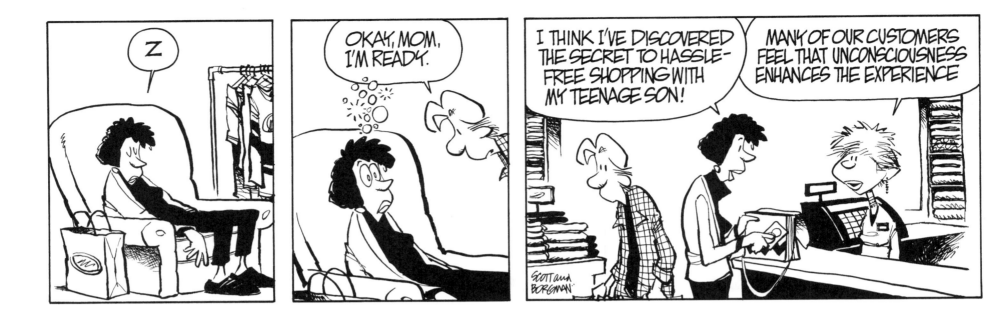

I'm a mother to three boys; the oldest is twelve going on sixteen! Many a day I have stood perplexed, like Connie Duncan has, as I watched my son vacillate between adolescence and teenhood, and between wanting the security of home and the independence of "the world out there."

Just when I think I'm losing my mind when I remind my son one more time to pick up his shoes or not eat ten minutes before dinner, or when I walk into his room and see last week's clean laundry piled on top of an old bowl of cereal, I pick up one of the many *Zits* books we have and thumb through it. I'm suddenly calmed by a sense of knowing that, cartoon or not, we parents have a common bond and that maybe, just maybe, it's all "normal for the condition"! Now I realize the more things change, the more they really do stay the same. I was exactly like that as a teen and so was my husband. Our children's children will also be as well. As much as I loved my mom, I would have died a thousand deaths if I had hung out with her on a Saturday night or, God forbid, if she had tried to relate to any of my friends!

S. S.

Jerry: I also write the comic strip *Baby Blues* (drawn by Rick Kirkman). This gives me the opportunity to write from both ends of the childhood years. And once in a while I can make those ends meet.

72

Jerry: Straight from my living room to the comics page. Our phones hide in so many weird and unlikely places that I never know where to look for them. Not that I ever get any phone calls anyway.

Jim: My wife labeled our handsets Kitchen, Bedroom, TV Room, and so on. She should have labeled them Under The Couch, Behind The Computer, and In The Laundry Pile to be more accurate.

Jim: Both Connie and Jeremy got new hairstyles in the course of our first decade. Here you see Jeremy sporting his original "rooster comb" hairstyle, but Mom got her curly hair early in year two. Her original straight black hair looked too severe.

81

83

Jerry: As a guy, I think the way Jim drew this is hilarious. As the father of a teenage girl, it terrifies me.

Jim: It isn't anything we do in particular that annoys our kids, it's our mere existence.

Jerry: Nothing changes the dynamic of a well-run household faster than an idle teenager. And usually not for the better.

Jim: We do a lot of writing-on-arm strips. In one of my favorites, Dad has to drive Jeremy down to Kinko's to copy the notes on his hands before he can wash them for dinner.

Jim: This happened in my house almost word-for-word, except that Jerry furnished the perfect pithy punch line for the strip. I wish he would follow me around and write great comebacks for me when I'm arguing with my kids.

Jerry: This is a great example of what a comic strip can do that a TV show can't. If Jeremy is giving a meandering explanation, we can make it actually meander.

Jerry: As parents we have to choose the battles we wish to fight with our kids. Some are just not winnable.

Jim: In Cincinnati where I live, we also do battle over shorts in the winter. If the snow is less than six inches deep, fifteen-year-olds think it's time to wear shorts to school.

Jim: Jerry and I work in different parts of the country but we talk for a long time each morning. One of my main functions on the strip is to stop Jerry when he says something funny and tell him to "write that down." "Party Doppler" was one of those lines.

Jim: Embedded in our family folklore is the notion that one of my children was conceived "while the blueberry muffins burned." We gave that line to Hector and gave guitarist Jeremy an even more disturbing association.

Jerry: We make a conscious effort to keep the comic strip playing field level. Score one for Mom.

Jim: What is it about teenagers and their messy rooms that drive parents crazy? Maybe it's the one parcel of turf they can control this side of their school locker, and they'll keep it exactly the opposite of the way we'd like it.

When I was growing up, clutter was not an option in my home, but my mom did make the fatal mistake of telling my brother and me we could paint our room any color we wanted. We chose black with neon yellow woodwork. But that's another story.

113

114

116

Jerry: After a day at the barn with my daughter and her horse, my mind started making connections, and, well . . .

Jim: We still get letters from moms telling us this is their all-time favorite. (Sniff!)

Jerry: This one would have made more sense if Jeremy's line had been "How many *feet* in a load."

To whom it may concern,

I just want to let you all know that I love your comic strips. I am really a twenty-five-year-old but I will forever be sixteen. Reading *Zits* is just pure heaven for me. I always look forward to new issues and I always check Barnes and Noble to see if anything new is out. It's my Harry Potter, you know.

Keep up the good work and laughs. I love *Zits*!

Thanks,
K.

P.S. If I were sixteen again and had gone to school with Jeremy, I would have totally had a crush on him.

127

128

Jim: *Zits* runs in family newspapers everywhere, so we must abide by the rules of the road. But let me tell you, doing a comic strip about a teenage boy without mentioning sex is like trying to write *Moby Dick* without mentioning whales.

Jerry: Is it just mine, or do your kids expend twice the energy to avoid a chore than it would have taken to just do it?

Jim: There are a few things in life you really should pay someone else to do—and one of them is teaching your kid to drive. But most states now require that parents spend fifty hours in the passenger seat next to their young learner, which is more cardio workout than most of us get at the gym.

Jerry: One of the great pleasures of working with Jim Borgman is that he can draw anything. I'm an artist, too, but this drawing would have killed me.

139

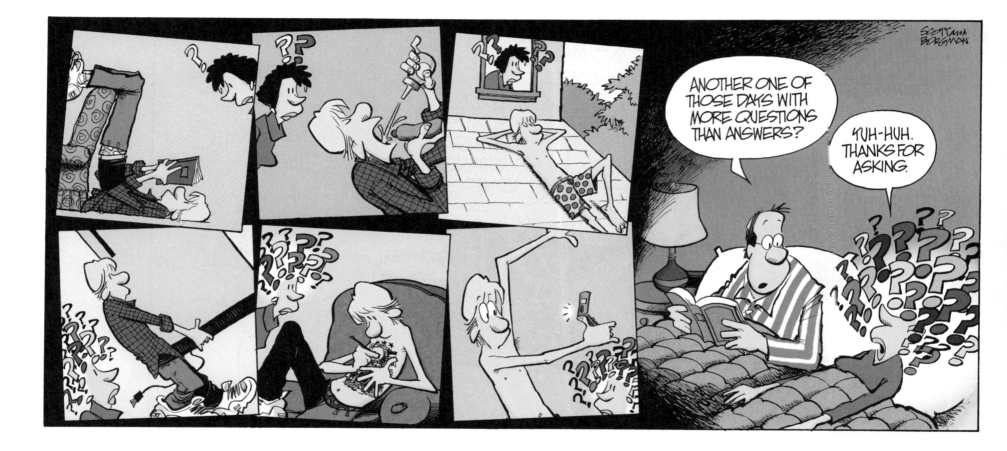

Jim: I love to give my wife foot rubs in the presence of our teenagers because their eyes roll so comically.

Jerry: Jeremy's mom and dad may not be perfect parents, but one thing they do get right is that they always present a united front. Because they act as a team, Jeremy can bounce against that wall of authority without being in danger of falling through a crack.

Jim: After seeing this in print, I promise never to dress Mom like a mime again.

SLAM!

SLAM!

SLAM!

I SUPPOSE THERE'S NO NEED FOR ME TO ASK HOW THE CLOTHES SHOPPING TRIP WENT.

NOT UNTIL THIS GLASS IS EMPTY.

I CAN'T FIGURE OUT WHY MY RIGHT LEG IS SO SORE.

IT'S JEREMY'S DRIVING LESSONS.

HOW COULD GIVING JEREMY DRIVING LESSONS GIVE ME A SORE--

SLOW DOWN!

BRAKE! BRAKE! BRAKE!

STOMP! STOMP! STOMP!

OH YEAH.

IT PROBABLY EXPLAINS WHY YOU'VE BEEN GRINDING YOUR TEETH AT NIGHT, TOO.

Jerry: Parenting must have been so easy before cell phones . . .

159

Jerry: What's up with that goofy sweater Mom wore for a while?

Jim: . . . and a really long foot rub.

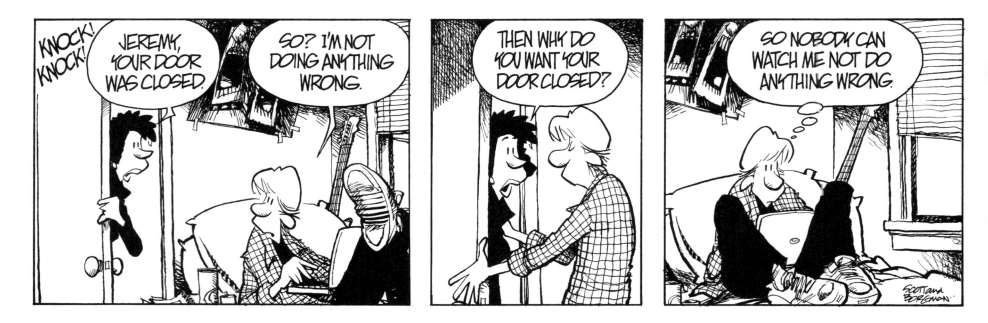

Jim: We receive an uncanny number of e-mails and letters from readers telling us that what we drew in *Zits* just happened in their house. It leaves us all a bit baffled—we sure don't know how we're doing it, either. Maybe this stuff is so universal that we can't help but hit you where you live.

168

Jerry: Another strip ripped from the fabric of my life. A whole generation raised on caffeine and sushi seemed funny to me. Funny and alarming, come to think of it.

Jim: I'm lucky—my mom is still going strong at eighty-five, so I've had time to catch up on my thank-yous. Still, if I lend her a postage stamp, she'll insist on paying me back. Mom, you sent me through college. Keep the forty-one cents.

Jerry: Attitude. It's part of the wardrobe in high school. The essential accessory.

180

Your cartoon series Zits has been more valuable to my husband and me in understanding our teenage boy than any counselor or psychiatrist ever could be, and believe me, we've been there. You have captured our teenager's angst, self-centeredness, ennui with all things nontechnological, and disdain of his parents to a "T." I work in a medical office where four of us are mothers of teenage sons. It is a daily ritual for us to read, enjoy, and roll our eyes at your comic strip. We can't believe your incisiveness. Your Christmas Eve strip of Jeremy's "Last Minute Gift Cards" deserves the equivalent of an Oscar for comic strips. You have elevated the essence of male teenhood to a new level. Thank you for the humor but also the understanding you have brought us. For my birthday tonight, my eighteen-year-old son gave me one of your books and I am thrilled to have my own collection to remind me what I will be missing when my son goes away to college in September.

Keep up the good work.

Sincerely,
F. L.

183

Jim: My daughter, the one who got the sleeping gene, sets four alarm clocks on school days.

Jerry: I like putting Jeremy in the middle of piles of clutter. It's cathartic because I come from a long line of neatniks. Our family crest features a can of scouring powder and a dust mop.

191

COULD MY PARENTS GET ANY DUMBER?

COULD MY PARENTS GET ANY DUMBER?

Jim: When you're not needed, you're not wanted. But when you are needed, your lap had better be ready.

200

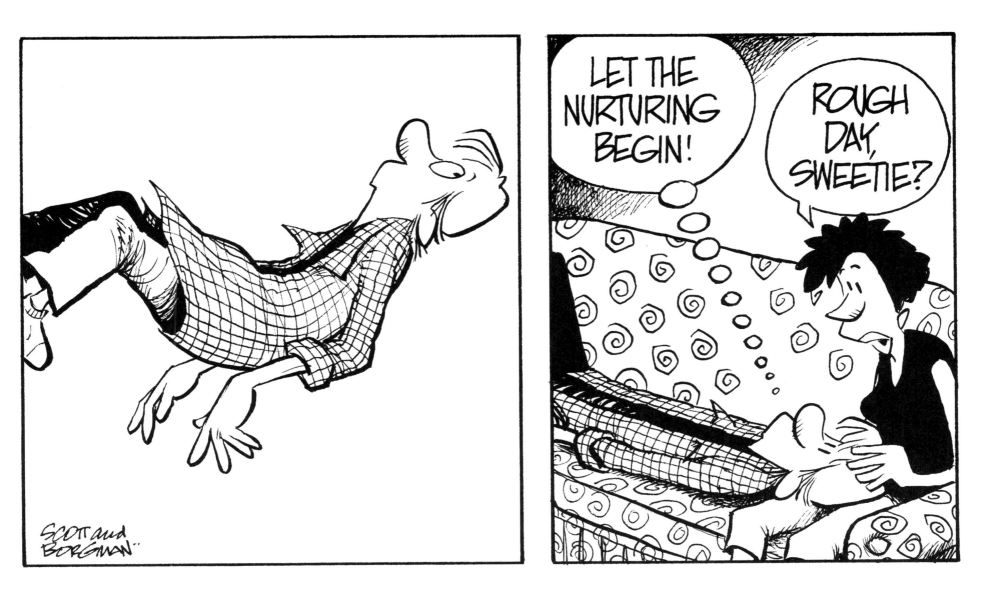

Jim: We sent Jeremy away for a week just to see what his folks would do . . .

. . . and they surprised us. This one made the suits at the syndicate nervous, but parents loved it.

Dear Mr. Scott and Mr. Borgman,

I just wanted to tell you that as a parent of a sixteen-year-old son, your cartoon lets me know I'm not alone. My refrigerator door used to be covered with cute, little pictures drawn by my son. Now it's covered with Zits cartoons cut from the newspaper. You have depicted exact moments in my life—from the dirty laundry in my son's room to the fact that his few months of driving with a permit now make him a much better driver than his mother. (I even had a fender bender just a few days before the one in your strip.)

Obviously one or both of you gentlemen have lived or are living with a teenage son. Thanks for the smiles.

Sincerely,
N. E.

Jerry: For cartoonists, *The Scream* is an almost irresistible image. There are endless ways to use it, all of which have pretty much been done. Here's my contribution. If Edvard Munch knew that his painting would someday become such a cliché, he would, well, scream.

Jim: We get letters if I fail to draw the seat belts on our characters in the car, but visually they're highly annoying.

211

Jerry: *Zits* currently appears worldwide in over 1,600 newspapers in 45 countries and 15 languages. I recently gave a speech in Norway about *Zits*, and I started out by showing this strip. It's always gratifying to get a laugh in another language.

Jim: As the designated launderer in our family, I only had to get buried under a mountain of dirty clothes a couple of times before I offered the kids two extra bucks on their weekly allowance to do their own. Best money I ever spent.

216

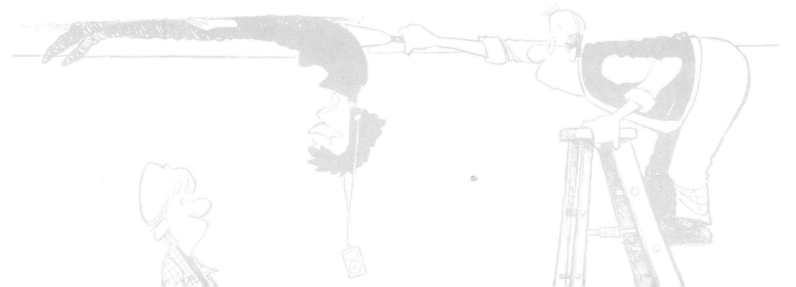

Jim: Mom has a wonderfully expressive face.

Jim: The scowling kid on the left perfectly embodies the prevailing teen attitude at these school functions. The pasty-looking dad is modeled after my buddy Jerry.

221

223

Dear Mr. Borgman and Mr. Scott,

I want to compliment you on your comic strip *Zits*. It has become very meaningful to my family. My son is in the eleventh grade . . . he's smart, smart mouthed, and has all the teen angst and things you can imagine. My husband was so stressed about his attitude. Then I started reading *Zits*. In the morning, I cut the strip out and paste it to my son's door before I leave for work so he sees it when he gets home. I show each one to my husband and I hear a sigh of relief: "You mean there are other kids like this out there?" It's been fun using your comic strip as a means of communication with a sixteen-year-old and with a fifty-eight-year-old. I just wanted you to know that there really is more to your strip than meets the eye. It has the potential to help parents understand more about their kids . . . and to have a laugh while doing it. Thanks. You are excellent at what you do.

N. F.

Jim: Teenagers portray some outrageous version of their alter egos on social networking sites, to the horror of parents who think only of the potential employers and admissions directors who will see them.

Jerry: I like doing visuals like this. It's perfectly clear that Jeremy's thoughts are completely overriding whatever it is that his mom is saying in this strip. No disrespect, just reality.

Jim: Connie's one flaw as a mother is that 99 percent of the time she forgets she has a second son away at college. Or maybe it's just us creators.

235

237

Jerry: Jeremy's shoes have been a major character in *Zits* since the beginning. They're probably the next most important characters after Pierce and way ahead of Jeremy's older brother, What's-His-Name.